RIDING ALONG in my AUTOMOBILE

THE AMERICAN CARS OF CUBA

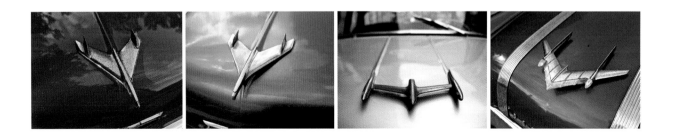

RIDING ALONG IN MY AUTOMOBILE

The American Cars of Cuba

Photos by Rupert Truman
Text by Storm Thorgerson
Producer Del Rowe

Foreword

by Nick Mason

What Storm knows about cars is minimal - and that's being kind. I know this because he's asked me to write this foreword. He knows I'm a fully paid up petrol head but clearly doesn't realise that, although I can reel off arcane information such as the firing order of the 1962 Ferrari 250 GTO (it's 1 7 5 11 3 9 6 12 2 8 4 10... since you ask), I know absolutely nothing about 'Big Yanks' from the 1950s.

Having said that, in 1966 I drove a 1957 Cadillac from Kentucky to Acapulco. It's probably worth noting that I have resisted ownership of anything similar for the subsequent 45 years. In fact, my own view is that these machines are best used static at the local drive-in cinema. With bench seat, steering column gear change and air conditioning nothing beats them in the social interaction stakes... whereas on the road their eco-credentials are somewhat nearer to a coal fired power station; seat belts and airbags a distant dream, and drivability would be laughable were it not so frightening.

However, I can't fail to be impressed by these pictures and what they tell us. Firstly I have to say how much I admire the ability of all the Cuban mechanics who manage to keep these Jurassic machines operational. In the 21st century, where any mechanical item that fails to work is simply removed and replaced, I still appreciate the extraordinary ingenuity of the men who fettle these leviathans and keep them on the streets. I doubt that a genuine factory replacement part has been seen for generations.

And I have to concede they look absolutely wonderful. This was a golden era of automotive design madness. It was all about sculptured chrome fenders, huge swooping curves, and totally unnecessary fins. Despite all their failings, no one could look at these pictures without feeling a tinge of regret for a bygone era.

These amazing looking cars really should be preserved for as long as possible, but given that they are doomed to meet their end in a breakers yard, it is particularly good that they have been so beautifully recorded in this book for posterity. Maybe I might even need one myself!

Riding Along In My Automobile

Published by StormStudios 2012

Concept by Storm Thorgerson
Photography by Rupert Truman
Text by Storm Thorgerson and Virgilio Ponce
Produced by Del Rowe
Design by Silvia Ruga and Storm Thorgerson
Computer Retouching by Lee Baker
Paintings by Duggie Fields
Researches by Charlotte Barnes

Dedicated to Trudy McGuinness and Barbie Antonis.

StormStudios are Dan Abbott, Rupert Truman, Peter Curzon and Storm Thorgerson
Lee Baker, Jerry Sweet, Laura Truman and Charlotte Barnes

Proofing by Hilite, UK
Printed by LEGO spa, Italy

Copyright © 2012 Storm Thorgerson

ISBN: 978-0-9570054-2-6

Introduction

by Storm Thorgerson

 **OT** ON YOUR NELLIE

You might as likely heard of the old American cars of Havana, Cuba - chrome and tail fin extravaganza as only American cars of the '50s and '60s could possess - what you might not know is that there are loads of them. You might well have thought like I did that there may be a few, an odd spattering here and there, needing to be tracked and located. But you'd be wrong... there are hundreds of them. Many operating as taxis, cruising up and down the thoroughfares, or holed up in a narrow back street, probably awaiting repair.

An extraordinary sight, reminiscent of a movie, caught temporarily in a timewarp which one would not even encounter in America itself, old cars usually replaced by newer models in the capitalistic drive for progress - no such thing in Havana of course - where instead some mysterious compote of necessity, passion, circumstance and loving care has prolonged the life of old American cars which ply the roads for trade or to show off, or rent to tourists; full of girls or driven by sole dudes, or ferrying tourist families and young lovers.

One presumes a sucbculture has grown up incoporating repairs, spare parts, commandeered bits, buying and selling, and black market pertol - since the majorirty of vehicles known as gas guzzlers consume vast quantities of fuel, not that the locals seem to be vexed by fumes whether ingested directly puffing on a ciggie or cigar, or indirectly care of belching vehicles... Fume City.

The roll call reads like a poem:
Chevrolet Pontiac
Dodge Cadillac
Mercury Studebaker Ford Fairlane
Oldsmobile
Plymouth Buick ...

Many looking like hungry sharks sporting grilles like teeth, elegant two-tone paint jobs often red and white, shiny purple and turquoise unexpectedly gleaming in the sunlight, jet black caddies sombre and ominous or shocking pink convertibles purr by....

There is always movement, often stately, as cars parade by gliding at mellow speeds down Havana's main drags. There's one and there's another one, an exotic procession of time machines... a wonder to behold, and not just in Havana, but also in the industrial town of Mazatalan, a bustling more ordinary place 100 miles to the west. Full of people going about their business or down the main drag of Veraderos; a hideous resort complex where gross eateries vie for space with outlets purveying the same tacky trinkets and souvenirs backed by new gaudy concretre hotels looking forlornly out to sea, and where down 20km of main street old American cars continually coast by and one can simply sit roadside and ogle, if one is of a mind.

But not for long... as spare parts get rarer or become too costly, or the political economics change and imports flood the market; or the passion withers and a new generation develops its own obsessions, the American cars of Cuba look destined for decline, sadly in some eyes.

**HY** DO A BOOK?

There are several books on the cars of Cuba and so why bother with yet another one? well... fanciful notion inclined us to think our book might be different; digital times called for a digital approach, both in camera technology and in Photoshop usage.

A fear that things may soon change and that the American car phenomenon might evaporate, and naturally rampant egos which persuaded us that our design perspective might bring a fresh perspective, but mostly because we adore old American cars and it seemed a damn good pretext to visit Cuba, whose music and dancing are equally strong incentives simply not as photogenic nor as time trapped.

ST Havana January 2012

Introducción

de Virgilio Ponce

Cuba is 180 km away from the United States and from 1898 until 1959 all its technology used to arrive, sometimes even before it was distributed in its own country. Seeing American cars has always been normal to us, we were born seeing them. Obviously after the triumph of the revolution, the cars and everything else which were coming from USA ceased to arrive. Even today there exists an economic blockade on the Great West Indie states by its big northerly neighbour.

The cars were always something which indicated the social group and they were not only a feature in Havana, but also in the rest of the country.

My paternal grandfather arrived in Cuba in 1910 and the first thing he did with his savings was to buy a car, take a picture of it and send it to all his relatives to show them that he was doing well. When my father was in business he had a small shoe factory. When I was born he owned two cars at the same time; my uncle Jose Izaguirre always had a car, an old 1946 Ford, which in 1959 he started using it as a Taxi, painting it in orange and black.

In my street (Avenue 31, between 56 and 58, Buenavista) only a few people had a car, I remember that the Galician Dario Gonzalez had an old green Chevrolet; Pedrito Prendes' uncle, Panchin Suarez had a black Cadillac and his mom, Santa Santiago, had a small German car, an Opel Record; the nurse who lived next to the bar, Tony's father, had a two-tone Ford.

Down the Avenue 31 cars were constantly passing by, of all types and models, so none of these vehicles would amaze us.

When I started travelling in Europe and saw modern cars and different models, I started to appreciate the old cars and above all the Cuban drivers who, with ingeniuity, managed to keep those old cars working for many years. More than just drivers they were mechanical specialists; most of the

time with only a screwdriver, a spanner, sandpaper and a piece of wire they would find a way to start a car that which had come to a halt. They would even use pieces from Soviet cars or tractors but they wouldn't leave the cars abandoned on the highway for long.

In any street of Havana you can find a broken down car with its tenacious owner working on the engine, changing pieces, adapting, polishing spark plugs, regulating platinum, caressing them.
A year ago, I saw a van with a transmission shaft made from the rack which distributes bags in the shops (neighbourhood market).

The cars in Cuba are part of the family, you love them, you spoil them, they serve as source of income (taxi), as well as for family use; going to the beach in the weekends, to the Malecon in the evenings, to the field to seek agricultural products and at many other times. They were essential for visiting the children in the country schools. They pass from father to son as part of the most precious heritage along with the family home.

Havana is the biggest rolling museum I have ever seen.

MACRO/MICRO

The devotion to preservation so apparent in old American cars is seemingly absent where buildings are concerned and not just a building or two but most of the whole damn place... Round every corner the city appears to be crumbling, barely a building remains unscarred by deterioration, mostly dramatic, as facades fall to their ground in random piles of masonry or weathered exteriors look as though they've been purposefully 'distressed' for a movie, and brick and stone skeletons loom in the early darkness.

Against this backdrop gleaming Chevrolets drive by full of cheerful Cubans - a sight of such incongruity one marvels again at the delightful weirdness... I guess maintenance of a car is a much simpler project, a one man issue, than that of a building needing a committee and an army of labourers.

BUICK

There it was! Outside my friends' hotel, gleaming pink and white, two-tone Buick convertible. Sleek and gorgeous, and best of all a serious looking dude sitting in it. All I could think was what are the little round portals over the front wheel, and how thrilling it would be to be riding in it, blonde in tow, wind in her hair, etc, displaying immediately my lack of any detailed vehicular knowledge.

MODEL. Special, 2 Door Convertible
MAKER. Buick, General Motors
DATE. 1951
PLACE. Flint, Michigan
PRICE. $ 2,156

3

PONTIAC

We were so taken with the double ribbing on the bonnet/hood, and the sleek lines of the side elevation, that we nearly decided to show both large, with no detail, but the color scheme within was too persuasive. From the chrome aggression of the front to the elegant side view, this Pontiac seems to sum up '50s America in so many ways... Somehow silver and red feel American to me, but I don't know why, and the double strapping along the bonnet like a large suitcase speaks of excess, whereas the two-tone color speaks of elegance.

MODEL. Star Chief Convertible
MAKER. General Motors, assembly Pontiac
DATE. 1955 (Second Generation)
PLACE. Michigan
PRICE. $ 2,691

CADILLAC

The graceful lines of this Cadillac, are,
I think, a joy to behold, and its length, to
marvel at! I suspect various elements on
the wrong side of the law also favoured it
for the same reasons, but of course they
wanted black to be cool, but I think this
green is tremendous. The Cadillac has a
stately quality, regulated elegance,
desirable, but associated with
undesirableness, ostentatious for
sure, but also a thing of splendour,
especially over the back wheels. It has
the customary flying hood ornament,
slightly more discrete and haunting than
others. A lovely green for the eyes, a
terrible green for the environment.

MODEL. Fleetwood, Series 62
2 Door Hardtop
MAKER. Cadillac, General Motors
DATE. 1952
PLACE. Detroit, Michigan
PRICE. $ 3,587

BUICK

What pleasure. A shiny two-tone Buick, sitting unattended in a side street in Vanderos. Could well be a taxi kept smart, at least on the outside. Similar to the first car in the book, the mysterious portals above the front wheel, and a front grille looking like a cross between a fireguard and an aging shark, again extraneous to function. We took a few pictures and crept away before the owner returned. We were no longer in Havana but in the resort of Vanderos, full of the other kind of sharks, one suspects.

MODEL. Special, 4 Door Sedan
MAKER. Buick, General Motors
DATE. 1951
PLACE. Flint, Michigan
PRICE. $ 2,139

CHEVROLET

This Belair by Chevrolet was a bronze, amber, browny colour, and glowed in the Cuban sunlight. It had previously appeared at the bottom of our hotel steps in the nightlight, but by the time we had got the camera gear it had left. We saw it a couple times more disappearing around corners, and so it became like a grail or chimera; a magic car, a car that we just had to photograph or the whole enterprise would collapse. On the one hand it is the pinnacle of the gaping jaw syndrome, but is also the beginning of fin time. The hat may be average, but the car was resplendent. Such lovely curves in the side line as it dips the back of the car - a beautiful thang as they used to say in Texas back in the '50s.

MODEL. Bel Air, 2 Door Convertible
MAKER. Chevrolet, General Motors
DATE. 1957 (Second Generation)
PLACE. St. Louis, Missouri
PRICE. $ 2,611

POLITICS
(about which I know not a lot)

In addition is the complex issue of politics... A communist state that is continually at odds with American ideology, disparages the percepts of capitalism and discourages the acquisition of American items and products - one can get Coke but it is Mexican Coca-Cola. Cubans decline dollar exchange preferring pounds or euros. And yet it seems that the most prized possession is an American car, albeit nearly vintage, but clearly American nonetheless, a beacon of capitalistic consumption, obvious like a toothache.

One can be forgiven for wondering why they were allowed at all, especially in the '60s when the new broom came out with a revolutionary flourish.

Necessity presumably determined matters - American cars acquired in the '40s and '50s were common and many Cubans owned one when the shutters came down... Practicality persuaded owners to keep their large impractical ostentatious cars going at all costs, no alternative being at hand, along with an emerging passion or love for these beasts of the road despite, or because of, their characteristic 'flashiness'. It struck me that the front grilles were either grinning or growling which reminded me of political overspeak, either totally false or totally aggressive, perhaps there is less of this in Cuba.

1. What's your name?
   - *Tony*
2. What type of car do you have?
   - *a 1956 Buick*
3. Why do you have the car?
   - *Because I like it, it is my life, without a car I do not know what to do.*
4. How do you keep it working?
   - *With what I earn with it, I invest it in maintaining it, and live well enough without asking anything to anybody.*
5. Is it expensive?
   - *The parts are expensive, therefore there is not, the mechanics I do myself, I am an artist, the taxes are also high.*
6. Are you going to keep it for long time?
   - *All the time possible, until it doesn't work.*

DODGE

If you didn't get it quickly... this is a Dodge, albeit with extra grille, door handle embellishments, light hoods like a croupier and other bits and pieces, but why oh why does it have a ram as a hood ornament? What does ram have to do with Dodge? Presumebly an expert would know the connection... anyway the wheels are too small, in my non-expert opinion.

MODEL. Meadowbrook, 4 Door Sedan
MAKER. Dodge, Chrysler Corporation
DATE. 1950
PLACE. Michigan
PRICE. $ 1,866

CHEVROLET

From the upturned wings of the blunt nosed hood ornament, to the interior dash, colour co-ordinated, to a grille of chrome splendour, formidable even; no stopping this baby. This Chevrolet is a delight, although I can't tell whether its green or blue, my typist says its greeny-blue (why not bluey-green you might ask?), which reminds me of Huey Green who used to compere a programme on British TV called Opportunity Knocks, though Huey wouldn't have known from Cuba driving to scuba diving.

MODEL. Deluxe, 2 Door Sedan
MAKER. Chevrolet, General Motors
DATE. 1954
PLACE. St. Louis, Missouri
PRICE. $ 1,717

OLDSMOBILE

These two pink cars were found, incredibly, outside our hotel, the Oldsmobile in the foreground is a slightly more lilac colour, and has extravagant accessories which were being added to as we arrived. Extra chrome chevrons were being added to the bonnet/hood... Is nothing sacred? You might think there was enough extraneous bits without having to add more, but I guess its part of the Cuban spirit, or attitude to these old beauties, for some it may be a proud possession, and further adornment, is allowable - though purists might turn in their grave.

MODEL. Super 88, Convertible
MAKER. Oldsmobile
DATE. 1955
PLACE. Lansing, Michigan
PRICE. $ 2,894

BUICK

It's the back door that does it. Looks like a flying trident, or a Viking spear, or some instrument of war from Ancient Greece. We screeched to a halt downtown and took a picture, ogling at the unnecessary flamboyance and by now customary reference to flying and speed. It seemed to us that whatever else was going on that much of the 'decoration' of American cars of the '50s and '60s, was totally intent upon promoting the idea of streamline and speed, and maybe even grace, albeit sabotaged in part by the excessive amount of chrome. Although the silver of the chrome works well with the blackness. We were fairly sure that the front grill was not original, so we paid little attention.

MODEL. Special, 4 Door Sedan
MAKER. Buick, General Motors
DATE. 1958
PLACE. Flint, Michigan
PRICE. $ 3,316

CADILLAC

Apart from the gaping jaws of the front grille, the blue and white of this Cadillac (I think), caught our eye. There are two more Cadillacs later about which I will write more. I'll let the pictures do the talking, for now.

MODEL. Fleetwood, Series 60 Special
4 Door Sedan
MAKER. Cadillac, General Motors
DATE. 1952
PLACE. Detroit, Michigan
PRICE. $ 4,323

FORD

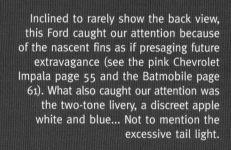

Inclined to rarely show the back view, this Ford caught our attention because of the nascent fins as if presaging future extravagance (see the pink Chevrolet Impala page 55 and the Batmobile page 61). What also caught our attention was the two-tone livery, a discreet apple white and blue... Not to mention the excessive tail light.

MODEL. Fairlane 500
4 Door two-tone Victoria
MAKER. Ford
DATE. 1958 (Second Generation)
PLACE. Claycomo, Missouri
PRICE. $ 2,605

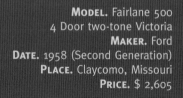

CHRYSLER

Stranger than fiction. This black monster stood out amongst an endless row of parked cars on the seafront, partly for its ugly grille, and partly for its phoenix emblem, and on closer inspection, for its strange appendages on top of the back wing, some projectile suspended inside a circle - its either a stoplight, tail light or indicator - we weren't too sure, reminiscent of something on a boat, which might accommodate wave motion, but on a car, appeared incongruous to say the least, although sadly to say the pothole strewn streets of Havana can give you a rough ride.

MODEL. Imperial, 4 Door Sedan
MAKER. Chrysler
DATE. 1956
PLACE. Michigan
PRICE. $ 5,257

What drew us to this car was firstly an argument about it's colour - is it grey, apple green, light blue grey, etc...? On seeing the emblem between the hood ornament and the grille on the front I wondered if American cars designers had a little scruple in so much as the design looks very like the one on the next page, which is for an Oldsmobile, whereas here it is for a Plymouth, though the subject matter, a world, or an airplane back view are poles apart... or are they?

MODEL. Cranbrook, 4 Door Sedan
MAKER. Plymouth, Chrysler Corporation
DATE. 1951
PLACE. Michigan
PRICE. $ 1,841

OLDSMOBILE

I'm going to eat you, I'm going to eat you, the fake smile of a corporate executive who is about to relieve you of your funds, as this car probably relieved its owners back in the '50s. Again the gaping grin of the front grill contrasts with the delightful colour scheme and the elegant lines of the side view. There seems to be a representation of a part of the world on the front, the significance of which escapes me - probably because I'm unworldly. The front elevation displays, echoing shapes, circles and ovals, in surprising resonance.

MODEL. Super 88, 4 Door Sedan
MAKER. Oldsmobile
DATE. 1955
PLACE. Lansing, Michigan
PRICE. $ 2,505

NOMALIES

Not wishing to be pseudo learned the most appropriate word that comes to mind from our visit to Havana, is anomaly. It struck me as a place which seemed out of kilter but not unhappy to be so, itself an anomaly.

Not short of cheerful faces nor friendly people, but the gruesome shadow of poverty lurks down many an alleyway... There is a fastidiousness in their dress but not in their untidy streets, there are many grand and old buildings but many in disrepair, many balconies over which hang colorful washing garrulous neighbours and languid lovers.

There seemed an equal fondness in the local gentry for ice creams on one hand, cigarillos and cigars on the other, what with belching busses and lorries and dysfunctional exhausts - it's fume city alright and it may feel like an unhealthy place but Cuba is known for its efficient health service.

Smooth marble floors of galleries and national institutions contrast more pot holes in the streets than you can count on your calculator, and the most obvious anomaly are the American cars of Cuba which are often spotless on the outside but running on a Skoda engine within or more starkly the spotlessness is set against cracked and crumbling masonary.

Then of course there is the issue of politics and money - there was a fundamental revolution in '59 but will it be sustained as Castro fades? Will the pressure of economics or the attraction of commerce dilute the idealism. The world is fast changing, need I say, from the Arab spring to China, from Brasil to... Cuba? Circumstance carries the joker and things may change in Cuba unexpectedly, and the American cars - the anomaly of anomalies - may soon disappear, which is one of the compelling reasons we wanted to do this book. And we hope this book will became not only an arty thing but also an historical thing.

This Corvair is either extremely rare or unusual, or a fabrication - being a concoction engineered by inventive Cubans, more like European cars, of which there are not many either, which has the engine in the back... Could this said to be a non-American American car, beats me.

MODEL. Corvair 500, 4 Door Sedan
MAKER. Chevrolet, General Motors
DATE. 1960 (First Generation)
PLACE. St Louis, Missouri
PRICE. $ 2,038

35

PONTIAC

This black Pontiac saloon caught our eye on account of a missing wheel. We thought it looked great, but wouldn't go far. When travelling on highways, those cars that seem to need roadside attention were usually old American cars, so the phenomenon veers wildly from spick and span beautifully maintained chariots of chrome, to broken down monsters in need of repair, stuck away in back streets or gloomy alleys, or looking distraught on the verge of a motorway. The hood ornament was interesting, being an art deco Red Indian, whose head is made sometimes of chrome, sometimes of amber-looking plastic, and sometimes of fake ivory, but always with a fierce and furrowed brow.

MODEL. Chieftain, 4 Door Sedan
MAKER. General Motors, assembly Pontiac
DATE. 1952 (First Generation)
PLACE. Various locations, Michigan
PRICE. $ 2,092

CADILLAC

This blue baby is some kind of customised admix. It has too many side windows, it appears to have a back that doesn't comfortably belong to the front as if two separate cars have been stitched together, or even a separate top and bottom, not that we have any idea how this is possible, since it looks seamless. The front indicators seem to be on springs, and the centre lights have more chrome crossing them than actual lights, whilst the hood ornament has a curved wing and looks like a demon. Spooky. The only thing thats not spooky is its sky blue colour.

MODEL. Fleetwood, Series 62 Special
Custom body
MAKER. Cadillac, General Motors
DATE. 1952
PLACE. Detroit, Michigan
PRICE. $ 3,684

FORD

This red Mercury was the only Mercury we saw, but I was drawn to it by a famous Steve Miller song called *Mercury Blues*, in Fly Like An Eagle - such a great guitarist - and also because of the ornate house outside which it was parked.

MODEL. Mercury Monterey
MAKER. Ford
DATE. 1953 (First Generation)
PLACE. St. Louis, Missouri
PRICE. $ 2,115

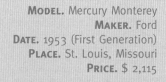

CHEVROLET

This station wagon is a severe anomaly, sporting accoutrements that seem not to fit, like roof rack and the sun visor, though there are other that do - like the elegant light hood and the petite indicators and then some which are in between like the two-tone colour and the rear wheel guards, quite sophisticated for a station wagon.

MODEL. Styleline Deluxe,
4 Door Station Wagon
MAKER. Chevrolet, General Motors
DATE. 1950
PLACE. St. Louis, Missouri
PRICE. $ 1,994

OLDSMOBILE

The wide front grille, as opposed to chrome, has been painted white, perhaps to echo the roof. The whiteness is carried on above the back wheel, again where one might expect chrome, I'm not sure of its significance nor of the significance of the saturn like emblem in the front of the car. The colour of this car has been said to be maroon, but I think its more of a chocolate brown, milk chocolate rather than dark chocolate. It was the only time I saw this colour.

MODEL. Super 88, 4 Door Sedan
MAKER. Oldsmobile
DATE. 1951
PLACE. Lansing, Michigan
PRICE. $ 2,503

CHEVROLET

We're sure that the front bar is an extra, but that didn't stop us from admiring this Belair, which was more than two-tone, because it's white, blue and chrome, especially on the back door, not to mention the very streamlined upturned winged aeroplane in the front centre of the bonnet whose ridge behind it reminds one of a vapour trail. More chrome than you could shake a stick at.

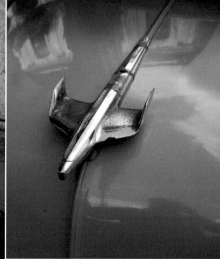

MODEL. Bel Air, 4 Door
MAKER. Chevrolet, General Motors
DATE. 1954 (First Generation)

PLACE. St. Louis, Missouri
PRICE. $ 1,884

47

DODGE

This red Dodge was parked in the main thoroughfare and had a most peculiar black and shiny bonnet, or hood, as the Americans like to call it, which seems shorter than it should be - God knows how you get to the radiator if its at the front. Never did find out. The hood ornament is abstract and somewhat more restrained than many others that we saw.

MODEL. Coronet, 4 Door
MAKER. Dodge, Chrysler Corporation
DATE. 1955 (Second Generation)
PLACE. Michigan
PRICE. $ 2,116

CUBA
MDB768

DESOTO

This is the only DeSoto we saw, being spelt wrongly and also of an odd lilac colour, the grille, like the gnarled teeth of a predator and a customary yet incongruous airplane on the bonnet. It was spotted near the railway station outside of which was a taxi rank entirely of American cars, and derelict engines. More incongruity.

MODEL. Diplomat, 4 Door Sedan
MAKER. DeSoto, Chrysler Corporation
DATE. 1955
PLACE. Various locations, Michigan
PRICE. $ 2,792 Approx

CHRYSLER

Of all the silly things I was attracted to this particular Chrysler was because of where it was parked (see opposite). Being a symphony of colour: pale turquoise against a pale blue background, seems the driver was colour conscious even when parking it. The other features of interest are the back wheel guard, the flying ring on the hood ornament and the strangely coloured roof, obviously the colour conscious owner partly lost the plot half way through.

MODEL. Saratoga, 4 Door Sedan
MAKER. Chrysler
DATE. 1952
PLACE. Michigan
PRICE. $ 3,204

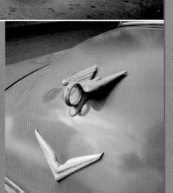

FORD

This station wagon would have had a great front grille if it had not been customised by a roll-bar, but it still looks from the side as if it had been stuck on a normal saloon - but what's normal for American cars of this period?

MODEL. Customline Country Sedan Station Wagon
MAKER. Ford
DATE. 1952
PLACE. Chicago, Illinois
PRICE. $ 2,249

THEORY OF FLAMBOYANCE

Talk of necessity and practicality may well be true but is not the whole story, or 'enchilada', because instinct tells me that there is a psychological aspect, in so much as American cars are not the greatest cars, in the Audi sense or even Jaguar or Aston Martin - they are neither performance oriented nor precision engineered nor as handcrafted as a Morgan - remember the most valuable car in the world is... The Dino Ferrari? or Facel Vega, not an American car of the period.

But what they do have in spades is style... No other set of automobiles possess such an idiosyncratic sense of style, a verve and outrageousness, a flamboyance quite unnecessary motor wise, unequalled anywhere anytime else, and my feeling is that this echoes and appreals to cuban sensibility - their love of show, of dancing, the colourful dresses and the style of shoes, mens suits. Cubans love the dapper, the expressive, and the flamboyance of American cars exemplifies what one likes, what one wants to ride in or be seen riding in viz a question of style - from whitewalled tyres to extravagant tail fins from bonnet marques to enormous tail lights to melodramatic grilles and fins of indulgence, a chrome frenzy... What could be cooler?

In some seedier way the American cars of Havana are akin to pimping, offering a sexy model to be seen with or given a ride in, or by, such that one wonders if there are protectors/pimps looking after a group of cars and securing johns/customers for the drivers and preserving their patch for business, prostitution being the oldest business they say.

1. What's your name?
   - *Víctor*
2. What type of car do you have?
   - *A 1950 Cadillac*
3. Why do you have the car?
   - *This is my work, from this I live.*
4. How do you keep it working
   - *This car is very cared for, was my father's before me, he did the same thing as me, I spoil it a lot as he did.*
5. Is it expensive?
   - *The petrol is very expensive, the parts since the revolution won do not arrive, one must seek them for the left (he means in the black market), so I spend a lot on all that, but is worth it, look, the taxes are also high.*
6. Are you going to keep it for long time?
   - *I will never leave it, this is a rolling museum.*

What a joy! A bright bright blue Chevrolet convertible, not dissimilar from that on page 71 whereas this is vivid royal blue with white steering wheel and upholstery. The windscreen divider, the back wheel covering, the brutal grille, and the elegant side elevation combine to make this a sight for sore eyes, glimmering in the morning sunshine. Mind blowing, if you like this kind of thing. (A picture of Che Guevara hangs from the review mirror, though I imagine he might turn in his grave at such American bravura)

MODEL. Styleline Deluxe 2 Door Convertible
MAKER. Chevrolet, General Motors
DATE. 1951 (First Generation)
PLACE. St. Louis, Missouri
PRICE. $ 2,030

A pink Impala and a lilac Oldsmobile were parked adjacent to each other at our hotel. It seemed like an offering from the deities to be within such easy reach. This Ford with its rear wings, streamlined side decoration, matching steering wheel, is a shocking pink - all over, which is of course fine if you like pink, I have to say as a rule, I don't, but on the car It felt ok, flamboyant, excessive, colourful, shiny, streamlined, fins, chrome, large tail lights, etc, etc, but it's not a Cadillac.

Model. Impala, Convertible
Maker. Chevrolet, General Motors
Date. 1960 (Second Generation)
Place. St. Louis, Missouri
Price. $ 2,954

I think this Ford is remarkable for two particular reasons. One because it is the widest grill in Christendom, and secondly because it is an unusual colour scheme, that is a rather unattractive light green which is strangely dirty, and a purple. It also has sculptured fins that protrude at a slightly odd angle.

MODEL. Fairlane Galaxie
MAKER. Ford
DATE. 1959 (Second Generation)
PLACE. Claycomo, Missouri
PRICE. $ 2,642

This pink extravaganza is like something out
of the animal kingdom, probably marine,
like a reef shark or hammerhead, but going
to a party not out hunting, genus vehiculus
pinkus cadillacus giganticus, Too long by
half with tail lights the size of flying saucers,
fins sharp and pointed like an actual shark,
a grill wide enough to occupy two lanes,
and a colour designed to temporarily blind
you from 50 yards. In every direction this
convertible boarded on the obscene, the
obscenely delicious I might add. I pity
anyone who falls suddenly on the back fin
or becomes impaled when the car suddenly
stops, which of course might happen
in Cuba, a country of surprises.

Model. Eldorado Biarritz, Convertible
Maker. Cadillac, General Motors
Date. 1959
Place. Detroit, Michigan
Price. $ 7,401

Rupert and Virgilio, our interpreter, jumped up and down with excitement on seeing this car, shouting 'Batmobile, Batmobile', especially the fins at the back, like the flukes of a whale, and I could see what they meant, but I was as impressed by the Chevron delta wing on the side of the back wing, looking like some kind of flying V- bomber, whose vapour trails were accentuated by the contours of the actual bodywork, so where light bounced off the curved body, also became the aforementioned vapour trail. So much effort into this flying metaphor, that it struck me again, the incongruity, along with the fins, hood ornaments, that flying seemed such a preoccupation of American car designers in the '50s and '60s, as if they wanted their cars to be airplanes and themselves to be pilots. Nought so strange as folk, especially designers, and I should know.

MODEL. Impala, 4 Door Sedan   **PLACE.** St. Louis, Missouri
MAKER. Chevrolet, General Motors   **PRICE.** $ 2,697
DATE. 1960 (Second Generation)

OLDSMOBILE

White roof black body. This Oldsmobile is part of the taxi rank outside the railway station, comprised mostly of American cars, no Peugeots here. Two particular features caught our attention, firstly the curved windscreen coming around the side and also accentuating the elegant sweep of the whole roof, and secondly, the strange tail finlike extensions, which look a bit like the back end of rockets. All that for tail lights?

MODEL. Super 88
4 Door Holiday Hardtop
MAKER. Oldsmobile
DATE. 1959
PLACE. Lansing, Michigan
PRICE. $ 3,405

CHEVROLET

In the dappled shade of a main street, alongside the main promenade which runs down from the centre to the sea, much loved for strolling in the early evening and skateboarding, and patrolled by prostitutes at night (Rupert and I were approached three times upon returning to our hotel) is where we found this pink Chevrolet, immaculate, spotless and in better condition than anything around it. There are in fact many Chevrolets in Havana, but none so bright and cheery as this one.

MODEL. 210, 4 Door Sedan
MAKER. Chevrolet, General Motors
DATE. 1956
PLACE. St. Louis, Missouri
PRICE. $ 2,054

FORD

Hard to say whether this two-tone Ford is more attractive than the colonnade or not. The white of the two-tone colour system seems to enhance the embryonic tail fins, which in fact house overlarge stoplights. Talking of lights, the front main lights have an overhang like eyelids, not to mention what my typist calls the funny looking thing in the middle of the bonnet.

MODEL. Fairlane, 4 Door Town Sedan
MAKER. Ford
DATE. 1957 (Second Generation)
PLACE. Claycomo, Missouri
PRICE. $ 2,386

05

1. What's your name?
   - *Alex*
2. What type of car do you have?
   - *a 1952 Chevrolet*
3. Why do you have the car?
   - *Because I inherited it.*
4. How do you keep it working
   - *I am an inventor or magician, only because of this I can maintain it. Since I was born I helped my father with the cars.*
5. Is it expensive?
   - *Here all is expensive and to maintain a car that is not Russian costs a lot, and the gasoline is sky high expensive.*
6. Are you going to keep it for long time?
   - *Never I have thought to sell it, although if they give me a new Chevrolet and they pay me what this is worth, I will sell it.*

ESIGN

This tome is compiled from a design perspective... A delight in objects which look good, there is here little knowledge nor interest in what is under the bonnet - we are surface oriented and visual centric not much concerned, I'm afraid, with mechanical specs nor peformance data, only in how the cars look. Yes, it is the exterior that counts and what an exterior! Mostly exhibiting a functionless quality declaring up front that it is all front - not just extravagant shapes, bright colours, but numerous details from speedometer to stop lights, from flying hood ornaments to steering wheel centres, a preponderance for aerodynamic or jet age design. Items with wings and sleek tailbacks plus a wilful reworking of art deco motifs, a fondness for lines of convergence and any amount of decoration which seemed to add even more sleekness. Not to mention upholstery, often gleaming white and red ribbed leather or shiny plastic, matching the exterior colour scheme. It is clear that American car designers of the time were unafraid... After the Depression and the War this is perhaps understandable.

CHEVROLET

I'm not particularly good at dating, in any sense of the word actually, but I could easily imagine Gatsby to be driving this car, with Daisy sitting next to him, he in a chocolate brown suit and her in a floral dress, all style and elegance in their yellow convertible, arriving for afternoon tea in Rhode Island circa 1935. As with black Cadillacs in Chicago, though for entirely different reasons, American cars evoke both nostalgia and romance and can trigger an immediate association. Performance, questionable, character, oodles.

MODEL. Styleline Deluxe
2 Door Convertible
MAKER. Chevrolet, General Motors
DATE. 1952
PLACE. St. Louis, Missouri
PRICE. $ 2,128

CHEVROLET

The stark black and white colour scheme first attracted, but then the front grille, seemed to engulf the camera. We thought it might be a police car, from downtown Chicago circa 1950, but it was in fact, a taxi. The black and white theme was continued on the steering wheel and dashboard, and made for a striking colour coordinated event, like a well dressed man or woman attending a wedding. This Chevrolet is both elegant and monstrous at the same time, again a combination you might see at an upmarket or posh wedding where one ridiculous hat competes with another.

MODEL. Styleline Deluxe, 4 Door Sedan
MAKER. Chevrolet, General Motors
DATE. 1951
PLACE. St. Louis, Missouri
PRICE. $ 1,680

OLDSMOBILE

This Oldsmobile was also standing outside the capital, looking as though it might fold in the middle like some kind of giant wallet, and is full of extraneous lines of chrome down the side, presumably to enhance its length - you might have thought its long enough already, dear reader but not according to american car designers where lenght actual or decorative seemed important. Yet again the marroon and silver struk us as tipically american, either as a result of continual use or something from their red indian heritage. The partly covered back wheel is a coup-de-grace.

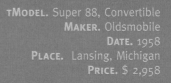

тModel. Super 88, Convertible
Maker. Oldsmobile
Date. 1958
Place. Lansing, Michigan
Price. $ 2,958

OLDSMOBILE

This Oldsmobile, seen in downtown Havana, sports a black and white livery but more discretely than the 'police car' on page 73. Its front grill looks like a fish, grouper, or flat faced shark, the kind of mouth that is actually bigger than everything else, for the avid consumption of prey or in this case, fuel. The hood ornament is art deco, thrusting its way forward in streamlined power, as if leading the car by the nose, or rather the mouth.

MODEL. Super 88 Holiday
4 Door Hardtop
MAKER. Oldsmobile
DATE. 1957
PLACE. Lansing, Michigan
PRICE. $ 3,257

PONTIAC

The amber and turquoise go well together, and I like the way the chrome side ribbing suddenly begins to turn up towards the front window, as if it had just changed its mind leaving graphic stars to mark its intention. Most of all I like the double chrome bands on the bonnet/hood like those of a suitcase, sweeping forward down towards the brutal grille, and sandwiching the ubiquitous aeroplane bonnet cap in-between. Aeroplanes again, say no more.

MODEL. Chieftain, 4 Door Sedan
MAKER. General Motors, assembly Pontiac
DATE. 1955 (Second Generation)
PLACE. Michigan
PRICE. $ 2, 164

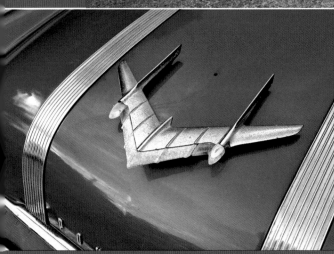

MODEL. Coronet, 4 Door
8 passengers limousine
MAKER. Dodge, Chrysler Corporation
DATE. 1955/56
PLACE. Various locations, Michigan
PRICE. $ 2,668

On our visit to Cuba we only saw one or two Dodges, and this one is a station-wagon in an attractive combination of silver and maroon, although I don't know if its roof-rack is original. In fact, the whole issue of originality is vexing. Clearly many of the American cars in Cuba have been customised, amended, improved. We actually came across a couple of blokes adding chrome chevrons to an Oldsmobile. It being difficult to determine this question of originality, we let it go, being more interested in how it looks, even if it is customised. We're fairly sure that paint jobs might not be original, but equally sure that in their heyday, American cars most likely came in different colours, as cars do today, so maybe it doesn't matter too much.

PLYMOUTH

The gently upward sloping back wings of this cream coloured Plymouth, caught our eye amidst the dusty streets of Mazatalan one lunchtime, when scurrying school kid mingled with office workers returning from lunch. Though we have digitally removed some fiery wavy design from the side back, as being irrelevant, if not a trifle ugly, this Plaza remains much as it was some 50 years previously.

MODEL. Plaza, 4 Door Sedan
MAKER. Plymouth, Chrysler Corporation
DATE. 1958
PLACE. Michigan
PRICE. $ 2,277

OLDSMOBILE

Despite the elegance of the wrap around glass front and back, it was the colour of this car, the silver and maroon, expressed so flowingly in the side view, which seemed more important. It wasn't just that many of these cars were two-tone, it was that these two colours were often displayed in long sweeping shapes, edged with chrome, tending to accentuate the streamlined quality, down to the hood ornament of this particular car, whose futuristic shape, looks like a precursor to Star Wars (did Lucas see the X-wing on a car in 'American Graffiti' just prior to making Star Wars?) A ridiculous connection I hear you murmur, but Star Wars is ridiculous in its imperial simplicity, yet irresistible in its characterisation.

MODEL. Super 88, 4 Door Sedan
MAKER. Oldsmobile
DATE. 1955
PLACE. Lansing, Michigan
PRICE. $ 2,503

06

1. What's your name?
- José, but all they call me 'Engineer'.
2. What type of car do you have?
- a 1946 Ford
3. Why do you have the car?
- I bought it, I changed it for an apartment that my wife had, which we did not use. I was without work, needed to work and wanted to be my own boss.
4. How do you keep it working
- I am a mechanical engineer and these cars are not complicated to fix, what you need to know is what you can adapt when you don't have original pieces
5. Is it expensive?
- As you know, Cuba does not receive anything from the United States, so if you can find an original part it will be very expensive, but I have always resolved the problem and kept it going, the gasoline yes, it is very expensive.
6. Are you going to keep it for long time?
- I've only had this car for 2 years, I know what it is worth, so I will never sell it, when things improve perhaps can buy another and create a business.

ATED

You may of course, dear reader, think that this is seriously a dumb idea for a title because all the American cars are dated but this chapter deals essentially with cars before the '50s and '60s. One of them is a convertible, turquoise, from the '30s and embodies, at least in my mind, a grand touring vibe as if coasting down the parkways of America, or else delivering an exclusively dressed couple to a party in the Hamptons.
There is something exquisite in the lines and curves which stays in the mind, like the best art nouveau, remaining graceful despite age.

In particular there is the Ford Super Deluxe - which took our eyes with its luminous silver color - and even better was the green Pontiac 'Silver Streak' which we liked so much we allotted it 4 pages, so beautiful from its hood ornament to its windscreen divider, from its monstrous grille to its two-tone green. And last but not least is the very old model A Ford, which we saw parked outside a house on the outskirts of Mazalatan like any old car for sale, exept not any old car but a very specific old car, but painted in red and not black, in open defiance of Henry Ford edict... "Any color as long as it's black".

FORD

An old Ford, but not the oldest, quite stately looking from the side though stiff backed. Right and proper. From the front the enormous side lights make it look like a monster, otherwise full of charm except the wheels which strike me as out of place, not that the whole bloody car isn't in modern day Cuba.

MODEL. Model A, 4 Door Fordor
MAKER. Ford
DATE. 1930-31
PLACE. Detroit, Michigan
PRICE. $ 600

I just love this picture! Taken near a roadside caff, some 30 or 40 miles from Havana on the way to Mazatalan. I could not but think that they had met for a chat. They struck me as talking cars, a bit like the talking engines of Thomas The Tank Engine fame - a series of beloved books by the Rev. Awdry - James Edward, Thomas, Gordon and others. Talking engines in some semi rural part of England, middle class sentimentality, but I'll never forget them, an indelible memory of childhood. And if you remember them too dear reader, you will see why I thought this picture reminiscent. I think it is also very much because the front grills look like mouths, smiling or growling, complaining about having to work so hard driving along (in my automobile as Chuck would have it).

MODEL. Super 88, 4 Door Sedan
MAKER. Oldsmobile
DATE. 1951
PLACE. Lansing, Michigan
PRICE. $ 2,143

MODEL. Bel Air, 4 Door Sedan
MAKER. Chevrolet, General Motors
DATE. 1954 (First Generation)
PLACE. St. Louis, Missouri
PRICE. $ 1,884

97

CHEVROLET

Just to show you how extremely shallow and fickle we are, we included this picture only because we liked the colour. It's got a nice central line going up the bonnet and up the windscreen and around the tail, but regrettably the grill has vanished in a black hole, as do most things; in a black hole.

MODEL. Styleline Deluxe
4 Door Sedan
MAKER. Chevrolet, General Motors
DATE. 1950 (First Generation)
PLACE. St. Louis, Missouri
PRICE. $1,690

PONTIAC

This Silver Streak is in fact a delightful two-tone green and might possibly have been the best car we saw, possibly, just loved its sloping back and rear wheel arch, and the shape of its windows all seemed to be in harmony, and in what I found to be a delightful contrast with the front grill, which happens to have one extra bar is an unrestrained riot of chrome, along with a central bonnet divider, whereas the windscreen is in two halves, it seems again to be in harmony with the rest of it. Harmony and disharmony might describe many an American car of this period.

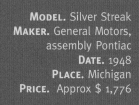

MODEL. Silver Streak
MAKER. General Motors,
assembly Pontiac
DATE. 1948
PLACE. Michigan
PRICE. Approx $ 1,776

FORD

The black side window frames, may well not be genuine but cannot detract from the wonderful outline of this '40s Ford, with its sloping back, windscreen divider, tiered grille, and a colour to die for. We found it parked next to a local bus, hampering our view. Luckily the owner turned up and moved it for us, as proud of his car as we were keen to photograph it.

Model. Super Deluxe
Maker. Ford
Date. 1947
Place. Missouri
Price. $ 1,440

CHEVROLET

What a beautiful convertible. I guess from the '40s, greeny blue with rounded lines, we saw it in a side street in Vanderas as part of a taxi rank, composed entirely of old American cars, which was of course splendid, but meant we couldn't photograph different angles. This is all we got, this is all you get. It seems the bonnet cap is a bit extravagant, a large chrome swan, I'm not convinced it's original, seemingly slightly out of step with the rest of the vehicle. I was going to ask the driver, but he drove off with a fare.

MODEL. Fleetmaster, Convertible 2 Door
MAKER. Chevrolet, General Motors
DATE. 1948
PLACE. St. Louis, Missouri
PRICE. $ 1,750

FORD

This very old car is sitting outside an ordinary house advertising itself for sale just like any old car, but it wasn't any old car, not quite the first commercial produced car Model T, but a Model A, which might appear in some other countries and in some other circumstances as very rare, but here seemed unremarkable... Other than I have re-marked upon it.

MODEL. Model A Sport Coupe
MAKER. Ford
DATE. 1928-1931
PLACE. Detroit, Michigan
PRICE. $ 525

07

LATERAL LINES

Looking for a common denominator of American car design in the '50s and '60s it seemed that their desire to express or reflect the jet age was paramount and was exemplified by lateral lines running along the side of the car.

I suspect that these lateral lines who were mostly deployed to exaggerate the length and in some way to suggest motion as if that this was the path the car was going to take. These lateral lines were normally edged in chrome and might extend from back to front, usually singular but not always, sometimes they'll have a bend in it or a kink (e.g. page 115, 65, 19...) or might lead on to further embellishment (e.g. page 9, 41, 117...) or being used to separate two colors (e.g. page 5, 57, 119...) and even sometimes stopping a abruptly (e.g. page 7, 45, 71...). Other common features such as hood ornaments tend to vary much more but in the case of front grilles the variety is restricted to grinning or growling, usually over stated, monstrous and chrome crazy.

1. What's your name?
   - *Angelo, Angelito*
2. What type of car do you have?
   - *a 1955 Oldsmobile*
3. Why do you have the car?
   - *Because I had the money to buy it from a guy who was going up north, I sold a van that I had before*
4. How do you keep it working
   - *I have my mechanic, I pay very well for my car never to stop, and I do it myself a bit*
5. Is it expensive?
   - *Everything is expensive here, but if you have money you don't have any problem, everything get sorted, here what you have to do is working and forget the story*
6. Are you going to keep it for long time?
   - *I don't think I'll ever sell it, this is like a goldmine, with this I support my family and if the American tourist will come we'll live very well*

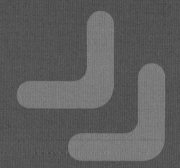

CHEVROLET

This Chevrolet is parked, I recall, by the sea, in the middle of a long curving road which forms part of the promenade in Havana with places so wide, there are parking places in the middle. Again it was the black and white and sweeping chrome lines that attracted, plus what one might call a buxom grill. The restrained fins at the rear presage the more extravagant fins which came later.

MODEL. Bel Air, 4 Door Hardtop Sedan
MAKER. Chevrolet, General Motors
DATE. 1957 (Second Generation)
PLACE. St. Louis, Missouri
PRICE. $ 2,464

FORD

Despite the roll bar, this Ford has some nice lines accentuated by the two-tone colour, and the shapes thereof, a sloping front, lights with overhang. The chrome lettering on the front side wing, seems to say Victoria, not that I have ever heard of this name before. If it had said Susan or Sally, you wouldn't have believed it. Is it after the queen or the owners girlfriend, is it a misspelling? Maybe it's Spanish for something?

MODEL. Fairlane Sunliner
2 Door Convertible
MAKER. Ford
DATE. 1955
PLACE. Claycomo, Missouri
PRICE. $ 2,324

CHEVROLET

One of many Chevrolets that we saw in Cuba, this one had a very fresh and vivid colour scheme, which Rupert caught as it passed a bus of the similar colour. This picture has absolutely nothing to do with cars, or Havana, just to do with colour and a coincidence of placing that us camera folk tend to enjoy.

MODEL. Bel Air, 4 Door Sedan
MAKER. Chevrolet, General Motors
DATE. 1957 (Second Generation)
PLACE. St. Louis, Missouri
PRICE. $ 2,390

CHEVROLET

Apple green splendour, outside a school in Mazatalan, again the great sweeping lines of the side chrome ribbing make this a delight. Further strengthened by the perpendicular window struts, nascent fins and yet another jet plane on the bonnet, (or hood as Americans call it) complete the picture.

MODEL. Bel Air, 4 Door Sedan
MAKER. Chevrolet, General Motors
DATE. 1956 (Second Generation)
PLACE. St. Louis, Missouri
PRICE. $ 2,167

119

Our attention was drawn, partly by its colour, partly because it was standing outside the old government building or capital, and partly because of an extravagant and absurd, large winged, very awkward looking phoenix or swan bonnet cap, that had it's wings out in a big V, but which I suspected was totally functionless, liable to snag, or cause injury rather than to perform any use. I think the dude with the hat is not the owner, but is soliciting for the taxi trade.

MODEL. Special, 2 Door Convertible
MAKER. Buick, General Motors
DATE. 1957
PLACE. Flint, Michigan
PRICE. $ 2.987

BUICK

We found this forest green Buick standing alone but spotless, in what appeared to be the rubbish strewn back lot of a block of flats. The concentric circles of the hood ornament seems to echo the circle in the grille, in turn echoing all the lights. One would like to think that the designer meant this, but such is the arbitrary nature of many of the American accessories (which is of course why I personally like them) that one is doubtful. What is also not entirely clear, is how Cubans, generally not that well off, could afford to run a car of this type, although this particular vehicle was a taxi, but one might think it would take a lot of fares to pay for the gas and to earn the upkeep.

MODEL. Special, 2 Door Sedan
MAKER. Buick, General Motors
DATE. 1957
PLACE. Flint, Michigan
PRICE. $ 2,596

CHEVROLET

Sleek and silver, wrap around windscreens, nascent fins, partly covered wheels and long transverse chromed ribbing, provides nigh on the complete package, including on second viewing, four little striped lines near the front light, indentations or chrome, bearing some secret code, I imagine. This beauty was standing outside a house with washing, they probably washed the car before they washed the clothes. One is never quite sure in Cuba how much American cars are necessary or trophies, practical or status symbols.

MODEL. Biscayne, 4 Door Sedan
MAKER. Chevrolet, General Motors
DATE. 1958 (Third Generation)
PLACE. St. Louis, Missouri
PRICE. $ 2,397

BUICK

Yet another Buick, but this time a Buick Special which seemed to contain an unexpected assortment of bits in addition to which it appear to me to be more bulbous, less sleek than other Buicks and an unexpected brownie red color. The odd bits included the head ornament - which looked like a cross between a missile and some kind of flying marsupial, and also the three portholes which contain relief helmets or two flying saucers, not withstanding a grille-like hens teeth or a gigantic comb.

MODEL. Special, 4 Door Sedan
MAKER. Buick, General Motors
DATE. 1951
PLACE. Flint, Michigan
PRICE. $ 2,139

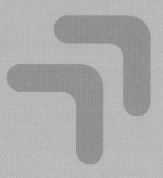

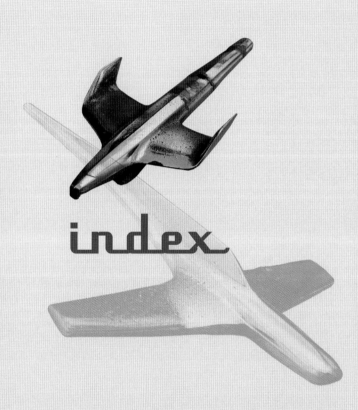

index